HOW TO SPIRITUALIZE
YOUR MARRIAGE

HOW TO SPIRITUALIZE YOUR MARRIAGE

S. KRIYANANDA

A How-to-Live Book
from Ananda Publications

Ananda Publications is a supporting industry for Ananda Cooperative Village, a community of over 300 people founded in 1968 by Swami Kriyananda. We produce and distribute books and recordings by Swami Kriyananda and other Ananda members on subjects of personal growth, self-transformation and simplicity. A free catalogue is available upon request.

We promise you prompt and efficient service, and will answer all personal letters with personal letters. Please feel free to write with any questions you may have about our books, recordings, yoga course, our community or our guest programs. It is our joy to serve you.

Ananda Publications
14618 Tyler Foote Road
Nevada City, CA 95959

OTHER WORKS BY S. KRIYANANDA

The Path: Autobiography of a Western Yogi

The Shortened Path *(condensed by the author)*

Yoga Postures for Self Awareness

Stories of Mukunda

Your Sun Sign as a Spiritual Guide

Crises in Modern Thought

Cooperative Communities

A Visit to Saints in India

Fourteen Steps to Perfect Joy
(A Self-Contained Home-Study Course in Yoga)

The Art of Creative Leadership

Keys to the Bhagavad Gita

Meaning in the Arts

The Road Ahead

How to Use Money for Your Own Highest Good

The Divine Romance (A Sonata for Piano)

Contents

Preface

By Susan M. Campbell, Ph.D.
Author of *The Couple's Journey:
Intimacy as a Path to Wholeness*
Co-director of the Institute for the
Study of Conscious Evolution

I n these times of divorce, heightened sex-role awareness, and family crises, we need to find a point of stability within ourselves that will help us to navigate these swirling rivers of change. *How to Spiritualize Your Marriage* offers a perspective on marriage that focuses on the enduring, *inner* qualities of relationships. At the same time it recognizes, and helps the reader to deal creatively with, change as an integral part of any ongoing relationship. By this balanced approach the author helps us to realize that change can in fact contribute to our spiritual growth.

This important book is for people who seek a deeper, fuller, more spiritual quality in their lives. Perhaps you have tried various avenues to personal fulfillment, and have come to realize that true self-fulfillment includes more than ego gratification. Or perhaps you are already guiding your life by spiritual principles, but would like advice on how to apply those principles to the practical problems of daily life. (How, for example, to inspire those closest to you, if they don't share your spiritual commitment?)

Perhaps you have been married for some time, and feel a need to revitalize your relationship. Or maybe you are contemplating matrimony, and hope to build a strong foundation for your union.

Whatever your marital status or stage in life, you will find insight and inspiration in these pages. The book explores an extremely broad range of topics—from sex to celibacy, from diet to energization by cosmic energy. It is a *practical* book, yet at the same time rooted in ancient traditions. With personal anecdotes, illustrative stories, and sayings from great sages, Swami Kriyananda sheds new light on countless crises that are faced by the modern couple.

In a final question-and-answer chapter he shows, further, how *any* concern or problem, no matter how mundane, can be reframed and viewed from a perspective of spiritual growth.

While this is essentially a "how-to" book, it is also a book of practical philosophy, showing as it does the relevance of high teachings to the very real problems of relationships in our time. The book has relevance not only for couples, but also for anyone interested, less personally, in the emerging holistic world-view as it affects marriage and family life.

Mill Valley, California
June 30, 1981

Introduction

Kriyananda has lectured, taught, and counseled people for over thirty years. His students, throughout the world, have numbered tens of thousands. He is the founder-director of what many people consider the most successful spiritual cooperative community anywhere: Ananda Village, in the Sierra Nevada foothills of northern California. A close disciple of the great yoga master Paramhansa Yogananda, Kriyananda is the acclaimed author of some fifteen books. *New Directions* magazine in Vancouver,

B.C., Canada, described him as "perhaps the most respected non-Indian yoga exponent in the world." Though a monk, his vast experience in counseling and guiding people in all walks of life has prepared him, perhaps uniquely, for the writing of this book on marriage and family life.

Ananda Publications
Nevada City, California

CHAPTER 1

Spiritual Marriage?

"They married, and lived happily ever after." How often have couples faced marriage with this romantic expectation. And how often, judging from the modern statistics on divorce, have their dreams been disappointed. Yet marriage *can* be happy—if it is based on realistic expectations. It can be happy if, above all, it is founded in a mutual desire for emotional, mental, and spiritual growth.

Marriage without *some* basis in spiritual

principles is like a rudderless ship: bound to flounder eventually on rocks of disillusionment and pain. But if the principles outlined in these pages are followed conscientiously, they will prove a pathway to as rewarding a relationship as any loving couple can be blessed to have together.

I believe I can honestly say, despite the fact that for most of my adult life I have been single, that I know the truth of what I am saying. As the founder of Ananda Village, what I have created is, in a sense, a living laboratory for the testing and discovery of what it takes for people in general, and couples in particular, to live happily and harmoniously together. I say, "couples in particular," because to my mind the success of a spiritual village depends on the ability of its householders, and not only of its monks and nuns, to guide their lives by spiritual principles. At Ananda we have created a community that has become famous the world over for the loving, joyful, and outgoing spirit of its members.

CHAPTER 2
Why Marriage?

There is a story of a famous sculptor in India who was asked by an admirer how he had managed to capture the shape of an elephant so perfectly in stone.

"Easy," replied the artist. "I simply cut away everything that didn't look like an elephant."

Marriage ought to be approached in a similar spirit. For if ever wedded bliss is to become not a hope merely, but a promise, one must exclude with rigid self-honesty every false expectation of it that one may be tempted to hold.

Society, unfortunately, conditions prospective couples to many such false expectations. Moreover, unseasoned physical and emotional needs often impel couples to make tragic mistakes.

I'm reminded of a couple who once told me they didn't want to go through the formality of a wedding because they had known too many couples to break up, once they'd solemnized their union with formal vows. Why, I asked them, such a breakdown after the sacrament? They replied that those friends, once married, had developed different expectations of one another—the thought, for instance, on the part of each that the other now *owed* him something. It wasn't the institution of marriage, you see, that was at fault. It was their false notion of what marriage ought to mean.

In this case, the right understanding would be that marriage, to be successful, involves an attitude of sharing, of giving, not of making selfish demands of one another.

I think there ought to be classes in the schools on how to create a happy and harmonious marriage. Wouldn't this subject be a good deal closer to the true needs of teenagers approaching adulthood than, say, subjects like medieval history? That is why, at Ananda, we have what we call How-to-Live schools: to teach children not only the standard subjects of "readin', writin', and 'rithmatic," but also how to conduct their lives for their own highest happiness.

The thought of marriage becomes too easily confused in people's minds with unrealistic mood images—a lifetime, for example, of candlelight and soft music, into which thoughts of dirty diapers, unpaid bills, and conflicting desires filter, if at all, somehow transformed by soothing moonlight, or by angels, into a lovely and effortless dream. Was it George Bernard Shaw who said, of youth's expectation of seeing the fervor of romantic love endure for a lifetime, "I can't imagine anyone wanting such a debilitating emotion to last forever!"

It is unrealistic even to expect love, as a conscious emotion, to continue unchecked, unthreatened, and unchanged through years of married life. It is difficult enough on the spiritual path even to love God—the very Source of all love—constantly and uninterruptedly. Spiritual literature refers again and again to "dry periods," when the devotee, though longing to feel devotion, can feel none. If this is true of the soul's relationship with

God, how much more true must it be of the fluctuations of feeling that men and women experience in their relationship with one another.

It seems to me that the obvious thing to do first, if we are to understand marriage without all the false glamour people attach to it, is to see it not as a thing apart from the normal human condition, but as intrinsic to that condition. That is to say, what makes a successful human being is essentially what it takes to make a successful marriage partner, also.

Romantics won't agree with me. They will allude to those particular features— beauty, for example, or (heaven help them) a dimpled smile—in members of the opposite sex which attract them to certain people as possible marriage partners whom they wouldn't dream of hiring as business partners. And of course I'd be mad to argue with them. All I'm saying is that the real *basis* of successful marriage isn't sex appeal, but the simple, human considerations that make for happy unions of all kinds—yes, even business partnerships.

For those, especially, who seek spiritual enlightenment, marriage should be seen in a basically spiritual context. Its deeper purpose is not to propagate the species, but to help each partner to achieve an inner balance.

This balance might be described as a union between one's feeling and his reason nature—that he may unite, ultimately, with the totality of Love and Wisdom that is God.

For man is much more than a biological animal. (I once said this to someone, who replied, "That's all we are: just animals." "Speak for yourself!" I returned.) It is one of the tenets—one might even term it a superstition—of our age to define man purely in terms of his biological urges. But we have souls—indeed, each of us *is* a soul.

We therefore were born with high aspirations—with a need, for instance, for wisdom and joy—and no human activity can fully satisfy us that doesn't take our soul hungers into consideration.

Consider a couple that can't have children. Is their marriage invalid because it is biologically fruitless? Certainly not. In marriage, there are soul-purposes that have nothing to do with biology.

What are those soul-purposes? Well, one, surely, is to help us to break the narrow confines of selfishness and ego. Other ways may accomplish this end also, but marriage is certainly one of the best. By learning to live for a larger reality than one's own, one begins to break the hard shell of egoism that keeps the soul from achieving union with the highest reality of all, God.

Another soul-purpose is self-knowledge. Marriage offers an objective proving ground for one's inner, spiritual development. For it is relatively easy to be gracious, friendly, and forgiving to chance acquaintances, but only in the close quarters of constant, daily association are one's spiritual qualities really tested.

I mentioned earlier the need for balancing feeling and reason. Many people nowadays insist that no differences exist, except biologically, between men and women; that it is our upbringing from childhood on that causes us to behave differently. Do you really believe that? I wouldn't argue that in our *souls* we are no different. But common experience, surely, tells us that even boy and girl babies behave differently from one another. Anyone who claims otherwise can only be trying to bend reality to fit theory. (And isn't that one of mankind's commonest mistakes?)

Dr. Spock, the famous baby doctor, reported that when he would lean down over little girl babies with a mirror on his forehead, they would look up happily and enjoy the images reflected in the glass. But when he leaned down over boy babies, they would reach up and grab his mirror, trying to figure out what it was.

Paramhansa Yogananda related the story of a conversation he had had once with a woman novelist. She prided herself on her capacity for impartial logic. Well, of course, to be a woman doesn't incapacitate one rationally! But this woman was saying, "I go *only* by reason." Yogananda didn't respond directly, but very cautiously steered the conversation around to the subject of a certain other woman novelist. Suddenly his companion began to lambast her rival.

"So you go entirely by reason, do you?" inquired the master, smiling. She had little choice at that point but to laugh with him, admitting that she'd given herself away.

In man, Yogananda said, reason is uppermost, and feeling kept hidden; while in woman the reverse is true: feeling is uppermost, and reason kept hidden. These differences don't mean that men haven't as great a *capacity* for love, nor women as great a *capacity* for reason. A man may, indeed, be capable of greater love than most women; and a woman may be able to reason more clearly than most men. But each *in his own nature* will depend more on reason if he is a man, and more on feeling, if a woman. It is only in the saints that we find a perfect balance. Yogananda was as much a mother as a father to his disciples. St. Teresa of Avila was described once by a city official as "No nun, but a bearded man!"

As we perfect our inner natures, we achieve a balance between reason and feeling, and between wisdom and love. Men become kinder, more compassionate. Women become more reasonable, less emotional. We all long, at least subconsciously, to achieve this balance; that is why we find ourselves instinctively drawn to the opposite sex. Our attraction is far more than physical. It is born of the desire to achieve perfect balance within ourselves. The more we achieve this inner balance, the less need we have to affirm it outwardly, in human marriage. The longing then develops in our hearts to attain inner, soul marriage with God.

Married couples who have reached a point of sufficient maturity in their relationship, and in themselves, to seek not only worldly fulfillment, but above all spiritual enlightenment, *must* learn to evaluate their marriage from a spiritual viewpoint.

They cannot depend on out-moded social definitions of marriage. Like the sculptor of the elephant, they must cut away from their ideas of marriage anything that is not compatible with their higher, spiritual aspirations.

Above all, they should cease looking upon marriage as an end in itself. Growth is a direction, not an already established fact. They should realize that the divine purpose of marriage is constant development, as devotees and as human beings, toward a goal of union that is essentially the same for everyone: union with God.

CHAPTER 3

Behavior
in Marriage

My guru's guru, Swami Sri Yukteswar, was wont to give his disciples
these simple words of advice: "Learn to
behave." Not, on the surface of it, the sort of
suggestion to be quoted as the wise utterance
of a great master! Rather, it may remind one of
that basically meaningless exhortation, "Be
good." Yet, on reflection, these brief words
yield a wealth of practical insight.

They speak, for one thing, to a common
failing of mankind: the tendency to expect

others to overlook one's bad behavior, so long as one's *intentions* are good. Spiritual aspirants often take the failing a step further, reasoning somewhat like this: "My inner life is Reality; the objective world is only a dream. So how can it matter how I behave outwardly? If I treat others rudely, my behavior is merely a part of the dream. Rudeness is all right, provided in my heart I love God." But my guru admonished us: "Do not imagine that you can win God's love, if you cannot yet win the love of your fellowman."

Our outward behavior, whether a dream or not, both reflects and, in its turn, influences our inner awareness. As an expression of this awareness, it helps to focus and affirm it; but as a denial, it dilutes, and may in time even destroy it.

Sri Yukteswar's advice holds especially true for close relationships, such as marriage. We are told that familiarity breeds contempt, but more often what it breeds is an attitude of simply taking the familiar object for granted. A person may be gracious to the veriest stranger, and yet overlook the simplest courtesy where his spouse is concerned.

I commented in the last chapter on the fluctuations of human feeling. Love, I remarked, cannot be expected to continue with unabated intensity forever. Let's face it, there are times when all of us feel that the world, including our own nearest and dearest, is rather too much with us. Marriage should, I think, be rooted primarily in *mutual* respect. For only out of such respect can love grow to become a healthy plant, capable of surviving all the storms of changing fortune—and feeling.

But respect can develop only out of inward centeredness—a centeredness not in the selfish ego, but in God: in the divine Self within. Respect can flourish only where a degree of distance is maintained, and an appreciation of each other's right to privacy.

For everyone needs some space of his own. A woman who once came to me for counseling complained of her husband, "He even thinks I'm rejecting him if I tell him I want privacy in the bathroom!"

Couples need time apart from one another—even as everyone needs time apart from the world (in sleep, for instance, or in meditation) in order to return to the struggle of life refreshed, and with renewed enthusiasm. Only from a sense of inward freedom can we preserve the creative joy that is the highest promise of any human relationship.

Remember, you came alone into this

world, and alone you'll leave it in death. The
effort to escape your aloneness by clinging to
another human being is based on a delusion.
Any union that encourages such clinging is
headed for the rocks of disappointment and,
eventually, of disillusionment.

I remember one couple: the wife so doted
on the husband that he, unable to bear her
suffocating worship, took to drinking heavily.
The more she worshiped him, the harder he
drank. It was painful to me, as their friend, to
see them drifting ineluctably toward disaster.
Nor could I say which was the greater pain:
hers, for doting so fondly on someone who, at
least by his present actions, was bound to
disappoint her in the end; or his, for the
imprisonment he felt in a cage of excessive
dependency which he could not, by the
canons of his upbringing, define as anything
but desirable and good.

The fact is, her affection was possessive,
and therefore far less generous than it seemed.
True love is based on mutual giving. It never
makes demands. It never says to the other
person, "You *owe* me such and so, because I
am your wife (or your husband)."

Love is a sharing, not a taking.

Marriage is such a sensitive relationship
that if in any way you try to coerce one

another, you stand in danger of damaging your relationship irretrievably.

Respect each other's free will. Instead of emotional commands and ultimatums, *offer* your suggestions kindly—humbly even—to the other person for his or her free consideration.

A body without a head cannot function. A physical and mental "body," similarly, that lacks the direction of spiritual awareness is bound sooner or later to stumble, spiritually. To expect to maintain an attitude of loving respect without a foundation in higher awareness would be like expecting a plant to flourish without soil.

In the Indian Scriptures the following advice is given to married couples: "The husband should love the wife, not for the sake of his wife alone, but for the sake of the Divine Mother who is manifest to him in the form of his wife. And the wife should love the husband, not only as her husband, but as the Lord manifest to her in human form."

As Emerson put it in his essay, "The Over-Soul": "I feel something higher in each of us overlooks this by-play, and Jove nods to Jove from behind each of us. Men descend to meet."

Hence, in offering as my subject the

spiritualization of marriage, I mean to make the point that unless marriage is spiritualized it cannot, in the deepest sense, be successful. The very *basis* of true marriage is a love that is spiritual, not earthy.

Respect for one another should include giving each other the freedom to grow and change, each at his own pace. Women who expect a second Jesus Christ for a husband would do better to enter a convent. And men who want another Sita* for a wife should remember that Ram himself made no demands of his saintly wife, but rather urged her *not* to sacrifice security and comfort in order to serve him.

A basic rule of life is to work with things as they *are*, not as one wishes they were. This rule certainly applies to human relationships, and perhaps above all to marriage. Accept your spouse as he or she *is*. Only on the basis of that acceptance will you have any chance of

---

*Sita was the devoted wife of Lord Ram , a king of the Raghu dynasty of ancient India. When Ram was sent into exile, Sita voluntarily accompanied him and shared his austere life in the forest. Abducted by an enemy king, Sita remained faithful to Ram through great trials. In India Sita is considered to be the embodiment of wifely devotion and conjugal fidelity. The complete story of Ram and Sita is told in the epic, *Ramayana*.

encouraging such potential as may exist in your spouse for improvement.

Would you like to see a change in your partner? First, introspect to see whether the need isn't really for an inner change in yourself. So, maybe you'd like him to be like Jesus Christ: Are *you* the Virgin Mary? And so, maybe you'd like her to be a modern Sita: Are *you* the Lord Ram ? As Sri Yukteswar put it, "Do you want to change the world? Change yourself!"

But it would be simplistic to claim that one is *always* at fault for any flaw that he observes in others. The Scriptural command-ment not to judge others refers to *disliking* them for their flaws; it is not a warning against developing the soul-faculty of discrimination. It is important for our own spiritual development to be able to see where the world is in relation to its own well-being, and to where we ourselves want to be on the path of life.

So then, what if you do see a flaw in your partner's character? The chances are that he has his share of them, given the average human condition! Should you try, then, to change him? If your desire to do so is rooted in love, and if your concern is for *his* (or for *her*) welfare, not for your own, you have a duty to try, *provided always that you try in the right way.*

It is seldom wise under any circumstance to offer advice. In the married state, however, it can be disastrous! Remember, you are not your spouse's guru. (Yet how many try to assume that role, where their wives or husbands are concerned!) Even when the other person *asks* for advice, treat the request very sensitively.

Never criticize. *Offer*—humbly, tentatively—mentally leaving the other person utterly free to accept or reject your offering. Even tell yourself that he will be doing *you* a favor if he accepts it. *Never* let yourself feel that he owes it to you to accept what you tell him.

Never speak under the influence of emotion. And never go deeply into a matter with your spouse when he or she is upset. Strong emotion abhors reason. *Do* plan to talk a difference out; don't suppress it. (It is amazing how often hurt feelings and misunderstandings, once one summons up the courage to confront them, simply evaporate.) But it shouldn't be viewed as suppression if you put it mentally on a shelf until the right moment to bring it out again.

Speak not only when both of you are

calm, but when whatever you say is likely to do the most good. Admittedly, this takes patience, but then, without patience no lasting good is ever accomplished. I have sometimes waited years for the right moment to say something that needed saying all that time. Had I spoken sooner, it would have been like yanking an unripe fruit off a tree. Usually in these cases, when I did speak, my words had a lasting effect.

An important guideline for married couples is to think always of giving one another *strength*, and not contributing to the other person's weaknesses. This may sound obvious, but it is surprising how many couples reinforce each other's negativity—agreeing with one's partner's dissatisfaction, for example, not always because one is dissatisfied personally, but for the more dubious purpose of accumulating credits against such a time as one may want one's own negativity reinforced. One of the most insidious aspects of marriage, if once one allows it entrance into the relationship, is the tendency toward increasing, not decreasing, both partners' delusions. In this manner marriage, which ought to be a means of assisting each other's spiritual development, can actually stand as a formidable barrier to any such development.

Think in terms of long rhythms, not of short ones. Keep your sense of over-all proportion. Remember that your commitment is to the total relationship, so don't get swept up in the exigencies of the moment.

It is easy, during a momentary pique, to forget how insignificant this feeling is compared to the over-all depth of your love for one another. Don't allow yourself, even by a sharp tone of voice, to convey with your pique the much greater (and, one hopes, completely false) message, "I don't love you."

If your partner is upset, *you* be the peacemaker. Don't play games with your love; too much is at stake. Why create a contest between you? If you can be the peacemaker this time, maybe he (or she) will play the same role for you, the next time *you* are upset.

Finally, don't make situations, or things, or *anything* more important in your relationship than the love and respect you bear one another, or than the spiritual support that you give one another. For circumstances change. They are fleeting compared to the long-range relationship you are building together—a relationship that may, if you build it sensitively and truly, carry you past the portals of this life into eternity.

CHAPTER 4

Sex in Marriage

A **marriage** is generally considered consummated when it has resulted in sexual union. This is, of course, a definition born of society's concern with its own continuity. But where the spiritualization of marriage is involved, consummation becomes primarily a spiritual, not a physical, issue. And since the true consummation of all human striving is divine union, consummation in marriage must be seen also as, in the highest sense, that sort of union between two souls which leads toward this highest fulfillment.

This point is important where the sexual aspects of marriage are considered. For from a social standpoint, mores limiting human sexuality are directed primarily at creating a stable environment for the raising of children. Society is not concerned with sexual abstinence within marriage. Married couples are encouraged, rather, to enjoy sexual intercourse as often as they desire it; indeed, one might almost say, as often as possible. It is the prize they are considered to have earned for having accepted the social responsibility of matrimony. But until the sexual aspects of marriage are brought under control, its higher goal of spiritual union must remain elusive.

Sexual union fulfills two purposes: It is necessary, of course, for the propagation of the species. It is also important as an affirmation of love. In the first case there is no viable alternative; all couples who desire children must engage in sexual union. But as an affirmation of love, sex ought not to be limited to the physical act of coition, and in this case particularly is only a stage in the spiritual development of a marriage. Couples who never grow beyond this stage are unlikely to reach that level in their relationship where the deepest love exists.

For in sexual intercourse, it is difficult to exclude a degree of self-indulgence, which is to say, of selfishness. Divine love, however, is purely self-giving.

Non-physical love between the sexes is often spoken of as "Platonic" love. But actually, Plato's ideal was that couples would come together sexually at first, and then, gradually over the years, refine their love to the point where to affirm it by sexual union was no longer necessary. Platonic love, strictly speaking, doesn't mean soul-love as *opposed* to love's sexual manifestations. It means, rather, a natural development *from* the physical *to* the spiritual.

Physical affection is a natural part of being human. It is also, however, the soul's destiny to grow beyond the human level. If one wants to develop from the natural to the supernatural and to achieve lasting, inner soul-freedom, one will need to develop to the point where he sees, not marriage only, but *every* relationship as existing purely on a divine plane — that is to say, in God.

In communities like Ananda, where close bonds are formed as people share together on many levels, one finds this spiritual relationship occurring more or less naturally. People come to feel brotherly or sisterly toward one another, regardless of blood relationships; they show less tendency than men and women in ordinary environments to see one another in sexual terms.

This happens also in marriage, as a couple grow closer together: They find it increasingly natural to relate to one another like brother and sister, or as good friends.

Such, however, is the power of social conditioning that what is perfectly natural becomes judged as unnatural. Let us face it, we are living in an age that places every possible emphasis on sex. Hardly an advertisement is to be seen for such essentially asexual objects as cigarettes, automobiles, or candy that doesn't in some way suggest to the prospective buyer that owning them will subtly enhance his sexual fulfillment. One might even say that we, in these "enlightened" times, have abandoned medieval theological dogmas only to create new dogmas of our own: for one, a *credo* that views sex as life's greatest imaginable fulfillment! And if you are married and can continue to enjoy sexual union until the age of ninety-five or a hundred — why, glorious! wonderful! Pity those poor dotards, indeed, who don't feel impelled to enjoy it daily.

Truth, however, has a way of finding its

way out into the light no matter how carefully
it is consigned to a corner. The other day a
friend of mine overheard two people speaking
of the commonest causes of divorce. "If it
isn't religion," one remarked, "it's sex!" The
plain truth is, *no* sense pleasure is enjoyable
when it is over-indulged. Stated more
positively, *all* sense pleasures are enhanced by
moderation. This is as true of eating, partying,
and good music as it is of sex. With excessive
indulgence, what may have begun as
enjoyment inevitably declines into mere
habit.

With sexual union, moreover, other
important factors require consideration. One
of these is the fact that there are *two* people's
feelings involved. One woman's definition of
over-indulgence may be her husband's
definition of moderation. But if partners fail
to take each other's feelings into account, the
sex act becomes what it inclines toward all too
easily in the first place: an act of self-
gratification, not of love; of taking, not of
giving; of mere supply and demand, not of
sensitive, mutual sharing. Between "having
sex" and "making love" there is a world of
difference. The latter may or may even not
include sexual union. The real purpose of
making love is to express deep inner feeling; it
is not the act itself. If it takes time and effort to

develop the ability to "make love" sensitively, the rewards are worth the cost. For the sex act to be truly loving it must be rooted in self-control.

Moderation in sex is important for another reason as well. Unlike other sense pleasures such as the enjoyment of music, the sex act represents an expenditure, not an absorption, or increase, of energy. This is not to say that to expend energy need necessarily be enervating; often, indeed, we draw more energy to ourselves by *using* what we already have. The opposite is also true: By continued disuse we may find that we have less energy to draw on when we need it — even as a stream, when it ceases to flow, grows stagnant. Thus, after expending energy in a healthful run one may feel oneself glowing with vitality; whereas, if one spent that time home in bed hoping thereby to conserve his strength, he might feel actually enervated by his idleness. To understand how the sex act relates to the flow of energy, however, it is important first to understand how it is that energy becomes awakened in the body, and even attracted from the very atmosphere around us.

Who, when he has performed a task willingly, has not experienced that he felt more energy than when he approached the same task reluctantly? Life-affirming attitudes of joy,* willingness, or love seem actually to *generate* energy in the body. Sadness, unwillingness, or self-preoccupation, on the other hand, seem to act almost like electrical switches by which the body's energy supply is shut off. These are matters of common observation. It may be that they are explainable in purely physiological, or in psycho-physiological, terms. According to ancient spiritual tradition, however, more is involved than using to best advantage the supply of energy already present in the body, or introduced into it by mechanical means such as eating. As Paramhansa Yogananda explained it, we are surrounded by an ocean of cosmic energy on which we draw also, to a greater or lesser degree all the time.

Yogananda developed a series of "energization" exercises, as he called them, which teach one how to draw consciously on this cosmic source of energy. I myself have practiced them daily for years, and can attest that they accomplish wonders. Among their other benefits, they produce a constant inner flow of vitality and well-being. The axiom on which these exercises are based is, "The greater the will, the greater the flow of energy." Yogananda taught that by a strong exertion of will, coupled with a sensitive awareness of the energy and of how the energy enters the body, one can tap into the infinite energy-source and invigorate the body and brain at will.

This manual on marriage is not the place to expound this teaching in greater detail, but surely what I have written already will find endorsement in common experience, namely, that attitudes of willingness, joy, and love are not merely the *result* of a healthy abundance of energy in the body: They actually *increase* this abundance.

As Dale Carnegie put it: "Act enthusiastic, and you'll *be* enthusiastic!"

When couples come together lovingly and joyfully, they naturally feel an increase of energy resulting from their union. From whence stems this increase? From the sex act itself? Is it not, rather, quite separately produced by their love and joy? Look at those couples for whom sex has ceased to be joyful, and has become merely a habit. Alas, how often such people seem utterly bored with life, and with one another; moody and irritable; prematurely old; and increasingly un-self-fulfilled. It may be argued in these cases that sex is not the culprit. It can be definitely stated, however, that nor has it proved the *cure* for their boredom and lack of energy. In fact, it is joy and love, not sexual union, that are the true causes of any increase of energy that people derive from sexual union.

To state this point more simply, *no* merely mechanical act that expends energy can *by itself* replenish it. The runner who jogs dispiritedly will return home exhausted; it is the joyful runner who returns refreshed. In the sex act, similarly, the mere mechanics of sex cannot possibly increase one's supply of energy; they can only, to some extent at least, deplete it.

For men, especially, the body must work hard to produce semen: that highly refined essence which represents the very cream of the body's inner productivity. When this inner activity becomes strained by excessive sexuality, the cream is diluted. The body itself, moreover, must then direct more energy toward the creation of semen — and thereby deflect energy away from other important inner functions. The consequences may not be observable at once, nor in clear (because immediate) relation to sexual activity itself; years, however, spent in such activity will result in a greater susceptibility to ill health; in nervousness, depression, loss of inner harmony, a decrease of mental clarity, and general lack of vitality. The youth who fondly imagines that he can indulge in sex with impunity discovers only years later the more serious symptoms of his self-abuse. By then he may blame them on a host of outward misfortunes. He may even seek illusory escape in ever more strenuous sexuality —

like a fish that seeks to escape the fisherman's net by burrowing deeper into the mud, instead of leaping over the side of the net to safety in the sea.

Young men, then, who think by constant indulgence to "prove" their masculinity, would do better to try to prove it in ways that will *reinforce*, not sap it. Such ways would include developing their determination and will power, or their ability to reason clearly. And for such development, self-control is a definite aid.

Women, too, suffer an energy-loss, though much less so than men. But in their lives, also, the effects — similar to those in the case of men — become evident over the years. A cosmetic company once did a survey to find out who, among various groups of women, had the best complexions. The results weren't anything the company could use in its advertising campaign: The single group of women with the best complexions were nuns!

The energy gain that people experience from sexual union is due to the consciousness they hold during the act — to their love, and their joy — and not to the act itself. Furthermore, this love and joy cannot but diminish, the more the sex act is allowed to sink to the level of habit. To approach a thing joyfully, it is necessary to treat it as something special, and not "have at it" merely because it is nighttime again, and you're in bed, and — well, *there* she is.

Everything in life becomes less precious — even stale — the more it is used. You may, as I said earlier, love beautiful music, but if you listen to it constantly it will eventually become annoying to you. Flowers are delightful, but a plethora of them easily becomes tiresome.

The Japanese make a practice of putting only one lovely object on display in the home at a time. A wise custom. An even wiser lesson.

I have said that it is by their love and joy that people find an increase of energy in the sex act. Well, then, — love and joyful sharing aside — wouldn't enthusiasm for the act itself, according to the principles I have outlined, draw more energy into the body also, even if it was motivated entirely by the desire for self-gratification?

Yes, in fact, it would. But here an important distinction needs to be made. For the grosser the thought, the grosser also the manifestation of energy. Energy that is directed only toward sexual gratification manifests literally on a lower plane — that is to say, in a lower vortex in the spine — lower, for instance, than love, whose vortex is in the region of the heart.

Have you ever noticed how, when you feel uplifted, your energy and consciousness literally seem to flow upward? Even your eyes gaze more easily upward. It is no accident that we use words like "uplifted," "high," and "elated," and expressions like "I feel on top of the world!" to describe our mood when we are spiritually at our best. Nor is it an accident that we say we feel "low," "depressed," "downcast," or "in the dumps" when we feel spiritually out of tune.

Energy that is limited in its vortex to the base of the spine generates in the mind thoughts of selfishness, cynicism, and all the other sad children of a wholly materialistic outlook on life. Thus, while selfless love ennobles the mind, sex for mere self-gratification eventually debases it, creating a coarse nature, and blinding one to all finer perceptions.

Let your physical union, then, be with love. And to keep it that way let it be only occasional; that is to say, let it *be* an *occasion*.

The way of moderation may be described as the way of nature. For, as Swami Sri Yukteswar stated in his book, *The Holy Science*, the sexual impulse has a natural, but also a diseased, state. In the diseased state, this impulse, like a fever, draws excessive energy to itself, demanding constant gratificaion. But in the natural state the sexual impulse demands but infrequent fulfillment. The major cause of the diseased state, Sri Yukteswar explained, is an unnatural diet: The toxins produced thereby settle in the lower intestines and irritate the sex nerves.* But there are other causes, besides diet, for unnatural sexual excitation. These were not mentioned in *The Holy Science*, perhaps because the author did not have to deal with a society as sexually stimulated as our own. Nowadays, because society as a whole is afflicted by the disease of excess, it is difficult even for people who otherwise eat and live properly to avoid the contagion.

Modern upbringing is the first culprit. For what influence is likely to reach children from an adult world in which hardly a billboard, book cover, movie, or TV advertisement misses the opportunity to convey in some way the message: "Sex is the *answer!*"?

---

*In his book — and also in my own home study course, *Fourteen Steps to Perfect Joy* — the reader will find information on the most natural diet for man.

The greatest hope for the future is right education. Children need to be taught to use their creative impulse wisely. Those who do so will find it easier later, as adults, to spiritualize their marriages. For now, however, most adults will need to proceed gradually, naturally, and with common sense in their efforts to achieve sublimation. Extreme efforts may, indeed, create more problems than they solve.

I advise "making haste slowly" because I have met many couples who, having entered the spiritual path, and having read in spiritual books that sexual self-control is the ideal, develop serious inner conflicts about their relationship with one another. They may indulge in the sex act in response to physical need, but afterward they feel guilty for having done so. The husband may end up seeing his wife as a temptress. The wife may start wondering if she made a mistake in ever marrying in the first place.

It is important to understand that you don't escape attachments by calling them ugly. You escape bondage to sex by spiritualizing and beautifying it — by making it more a communion of hearts and souls than of bodies; by realizing that sex is not only coition: It is a loving touch, a smile, a gentle embrace, a shared warmth that may require no further fulfillment to be fully satisfying. You spiritualize sex above all by learning to see God in the act, and then, gradually, concentrating more and more on *His* love flowing through you. In other words, there should be an inward consciousness of joy, of communion with Him, and of participation in His infinite love, even while making love physically. In this way, by gradual and natural degrees, you will find that you don't really need that outward affirmation of love for love to shine in your hearts just as strongly. Indeed, this is the deepest, purest married love of all.

You will never reach this point of inner freedom, however, if sex becomes for you something to hate, something to feel guilty about and suppress.

What about another alternative altogether — renunciation? *Ought* one to marry?

It isn't possible to make a general rule. For some, certainly, renunciation is the straightest and surest route to divine freedom. But I have seen people who at first wanted to live a celibate life, but who later married, finding that it was only *after* marriage that they achieved spiritual stability in their lives.

Always it will depend on the individual, on his personal needs. In true moral law there

are no absolutes, only directions. On the
spiritual path particularly, every effort should
be made to take people where they *are*, not
where some abstract rule or dogma says they
ought to be, and to develop them by natural
degrees — always with common sense — in
the direction of their own ultimate fulfillment.

Once you understand the direction that
marriage should take, you can use all aspects
of marriage to help you to grow spiritually. As
long as you retain a strong physical
consciousness in your marriage, there will
tend to be far more of the upsets, the hurts,
the false expectations, and the demands that
are so often the bane of marriage. But once
you spiritualize that relationship, you and
your spouse will find a real increase in your
affection for each other. As you perfect a
divine love between you, you will find
entering into your marriage a kind of sweet
dignity, a mutual respect and spiritual
advancement that will be, for both of you, a
source of perennial joy.

CHAPTER 5

Expansive Marriage

One of the false expectations with which couples approach marriage is the fond belief that they will forever be all in all to each other. I can't imagine *any* two people being that to each other—unless, perhaps, they are exceptionally stupid! No one person can ever help you to learn all your lessons in life. No one person can fulfill your every need.

No one, that is, but yourself. For all the fulfillment you have ever sought awaits you within. But that kind of fulfillment is never personal.

One purpose of marriage, as I said earlier, is to expand one's identity ever outward, from the ego to infinity. The ocean of cosmic awareness, which is God, has projected little waves of itself to become the myriad manifestations of worlds, atoms, rivers, other people, you, and me. We *seem* separate from that great reality only as long as we concentrate on our own separateness from it, and from one another—even as the wave appears separate only as long as we concentrate on it, rather than on the vast ocean of which it is a part.

To fix this image clearly in your mind, imagine the wave on the ocean to be endowed with a personality; and imagine, further, that in concentrating on its own separate and special reality it decides that its own, alone of all realities in the universe, is meaningful to it. Think of the wave therefore protruding itself further from the ocean in an effort to dominate all the surrounding waves. In so doing it sets itself in conflict with other waves; for these, too, similarly inflated with their own self-importance, want to dominate one another. As conflict builds among the many self-seeking waves, pain, fear, and suffering develop also.

The stronger the affirmation of ego, and the desire to advance and protect that ego, the greater the pain—and the more fleeting the pleasure.

There is no escape from suffering so long as one seeks his escape *through* the ego. The way to liberation lies in withdrawing the ego-wave back into the ocean—in realizing that our greater reality *is* the cosmic ocean. This expansion of awareness is no loss, though the ego may fight it with all the skill at its disposal, attached as it is to its own petty dominion. Instead, soul-expansion is the greatest possible gain.

Anything, indeed, that helps us to break out of the confines of selfishness and self-seeking will be for our own highest good. And since marriage is one means whereby man learns to expand his sense of personal identity, it has a much higher purpose than mere selfish fulfillment.

Marriage becomes, however, a barrier to that purpose if it is allowed to stand in the way of *further* expansion. "Us four and no more" was the way Paramhansa Yogananda described the mental wall people tend to place around their little homes, shutting the vast universe out of their lives. To those who seek the higher fulfillment of spiritual union, marriage should be seen, not as a cozy self-enclosure, but as a window onto ever-greater realities.

For worldly people, marriage represents a reinforcement of egoism—an attempt to buttress one's own sense of security and self-worth. But for those spiritual people who marry, marriage represents rather a reinforcement of their efforts at self-expansion.

Worldly people seek gain from one another. Spiritual people seek gain *for* one another, consciously or unconsciously with a view to realizing that the *only* true gain lies in expanding one's sympathies.

Worldly people think, "What can I derive from this relationship?" Spiritual people think, "What can I *give* to this relationship?"

Needless to say, the world is not divided on any issue into two distinct and easily identified camps. In some ways, many seemingly worldly marriages are truly spiritual. Whereas many supposedly spiritual marriages come apart at the seams on fundamental spiritual issues. We are all on the pathway to perfection. What we must concentrate on is not the point to which our journey has brought us so far, but on the direction we must continue to walk.

When I refer, then, with seeming glibness to "worldly" and "spiritual" people, please understand that my purpose is to direct your attention not to individuals, but rather to specific *directions* in your growth. The more your sympathies expand outward, the greater will be your own true fulfillment. And the more you allow those sympathies to shrink inward upon yourself—or, what is close to the same thing, upon your family in the thought, "I and mine,"—the more you will know insecurity, and a gnawing sense of insufficiency in your life.

An emphasis on universality, however, is not for those who have not learned to be loyal first to their own. The husband who thinks, "The whole universe is mine; why, then, be faithful to my wife?" is not yet refined enough in his perception of truth to be ready for *soul*-expansion, which is the only way out of egotism.

Such attitudes may be found also with respect to the spiritual path. It is found in the claim, "All truth is mine; why should I be faithful to my own spiritual path, or to my guru?" But "spiritual prostitutes," as Paramhansa Yogananda called people who can't stick to any path, never go deep enough at any point on the ice of life's experiences, on which they so love to skate, to penetrate through the crust of outwardness to the ocean of truth underneath.

It isn't only charity that begins at home: loyalty begins there, too. It is only through the window of such loyalty that we can touch the universe as we should—with our souls.

Through meditation and introspection, learn first to love yourself in the soul way, by sensing the hidden joy of your own being. Then, with that egoless love, reach out to touch your spouse, your children. Refine your love so that it becomes more and more pure; so that it contains less and less of the consciousness of "I and mine." Love your family as you love yourself: for their souls, not merely their personalities.

Then expand that love to include your neighbors, your countrymen, all mankind, all sentient beings—the universe! In this way will your love expand at last to become the love of God.

An outward expansion of love is what Yogananda called the social way of attaining cosmic consciousness. And a very important balance it is to the inward way of trying to merge with God in meditation.

And so it is that marriage can be a door to infinite awareness. But it won't be, unless you work hard at making it so! The obstacles to success will be many. While facing those obstacles in your struggle toward perfection, remember further these words of Yogananda's: "There are no such things as obstacles: There are only opportunities!"

In describing spiritual marriage, I want to emphasize this final point: that marriage, as such, is in no way a panacea; it is what you *do* with marriage, and for that matter with any human condition, that determines whether your progress will be toward greater freedom, or toward an increase of delusion.

CHAPTER 6

Spiritual Child Raising

The basic principles mentioned so far apply also to the question of raising children. Children, perhaps even more than one's spouse, are karmic incentives that force one to learn to relate *responsibly* to others—to relate, that is to say, in a giving way, eschewing the thought (so instinctive to the immature ego), "What's in it for me?"

In your relationship to your spouse, too, you are forced to relate responsibly. For whatever you say or do has an evident effect, one that it wouldn't have if you were, say, a hermit. Thus in marriage you are disciplined in ways that you might not be otherwise; in ways that you never are when relating casually to strangers.

For one thing, in marriage, you are obliged to relate to another person's ups and downs, and to do so meaningfully and sincerely. Thus marriage might be described as two pebbles rolling together down a river bed, each gradually wearing away the other's rough edges.

But if this is true of marriage, how much more true is it of one's relationship with one's children! After all, one can make demands, up to a point, of one's spouse. But how many can one make of his children? In tragedy, one's wife may give him comfort; but rarely so will his children. When facing major trials or challenges, husband and wife may stand together. But how often are children a help under such circumstances? More often they are a liability.

Children are a comfort, a joy, a hope for the future—many things, indeed; but a bulwark of strength almost never. And so it is that parents, in raising children, must learn to give—and give, and give! It is—like the challenge of marriage itself—a wonderful

opportunity: but one, again like marriage, that
must be approached selflessly, and with
wisdom.

In the divine scheme as it applies to
marriage, matrimony itself expands our
sympathies: first, by appealing to the desire
for personal fulfillment; and then by
expanding it to include the welfare of one
other human being: our spouse.

Our offspring, when they come, expand
those sympathies further: first, by including
more people in our own personal circle; and
then by minimizing our focus on *personal*
fulfillment.

As our children grow toward maturity,
and gradually wean themselves from the
family nest, our sympathies continue to
expand through *their* expanding interests.
Even thereafter, if we are wise, we continue to
demolish our mental barriers—until at last
our sympathies become broad enough to
claim the very universe as our home.

The struggle for self-expansion is not
equally difficult at every stage: from self to
spouse, from spouse to children, from
children to neighbors, from neighbors to
countrymen, from countrymen to all mankind, and from mankind outward to the
universe. Once the barrier of personal

attachment has been broken—once, in other words, we learn to expand our love beyond the enclosure of "I and mine," it becomes relatively easy from that point on to expand our love outward to embrace all men.

Wisest, finally, is he who doesn't wait to be *pushed* forward on his pathway to enlightenment by this mere natural scheme of things. Knowing the direction it is intended to take him, indeed, why wait passively to be taken? At any point along the journey we can decide to walk the path on our own strength.

We can, for example, try to expand our sympathies long before we have children. Why wait years to live *through* others, when life at every moment calls us to expand our own identity?

Indeed, the most spiritual approach to child raising would be to recognize in each child from the beginning, no creation of our own, but the stranger at the door: God, come to remind us of Himself, and of *his* love for us. In this way we will find it easiest to break the powerful hypnosis of delusion (again, that old "I and mine"), and to spiritualize our family life most perfectly in the realization that *all* belongs to Him.

Without the respect that allows others complete freedom to develop, each at his own

speed, and in his own way, it is all but
impossible for people to spiritualize their
relationships. Always there will arise the
temptation to make selfish demands. In the
raising of children, especially, it is important
to remember that they are already-developed
souls who have come as guests into your
family. You have a responsibility to share with
them your greater experience of life, perhaps
your wisdom, certainly your love and
protection. But you have *no* right to expect
them to grow up as reflections of your own
desires.

Most of us behold only the child. Noting
his innocence, we think he has everything to
learn from us. Yet who knows with what
wisdom a child has been born? "Trailing
clouds of glory do we come," wrote
Wordsworth in "Intimations of Immor-
tality." Perhaps even, as some believe, the
child has lived on earth before. Should this
belief be valid, his wisdom may be as much of
this world as ours is—even if it is a little rusty
in its application.

Education means, literally, "a drawing
out." To educate a child, then, it is necessary
to inspire him with understanding *from within*.
Well has it been said that truths are not so
much learned as *recognized*. And while the
child seems helpless now, during its efforts to
cope with its unaccustomed tools of body and

human nature, yet even during these formative years it deserves the respect and consideration due to a soul that is struggling, even as we are, to claim its own highest potential.

Indeed, as it is important to respect your spouse as a manifestation of God, so is it equally important to give that same respect to your children.

You'll have to treat them as children too, of course, because for a while they are playing that role—more deliberately than you may know!—of being helpless and irresponsible for a few years. A mother whom I know, in endeavoring to toilet train her three-year-old, tried shaming him with that old ploy, "Come on, be a *big* boy!"

"I don't want to be a big boy," he replied. "I like being a baby!"

It's a game they play, you see, for a time. And they'll force you to play it with them.

But just see how responsibly even a six-year-old can behave if his parents die, and if he is left to take care of his three-year-old sister. In many ways—and how astonishingly!—he will grow up overnight.

Children know more than they let on. And sometimes, in fact, they do let on.

My mother tells of how one day she was sitting at her dressing table, putting on make-up. I watched for awhile, then said to her in all seriousness, "Mother, don't be always thinking of your beauty, like Mrs. M——"; here I named someone who was, in fact, inordinately vain. It was an observation my mother hadn't expected to hear from such a little child.

Children do understand. But they may prefer not to call upon that more mature knowledge, perhaps because they find it more fun for awhile not to have to face the burdens that come with growing to adulthood. (Hence the perennial appeal to them of Peter Pan, the legendary boy who never grew up.)

So, respect your children—not only as adult souls in little bodies, but also as free souls with the full right, as children, to be childish, even foolish sometimes, and even completely out of control. Every age through which an individual lives is burdened with its attendant follies. Recognize your own, and give to others the freedom to wean themselves from theirs as and when they want to.

If you respect your children's freedom to play whatever role they choose to play, they will respond to you in kind. Parents who don't respect their children, who talk down to them, find their children's resultant frustration coming out, eventually, in the form of rebellion.

The principle, mentioned earlier, of being loyal to one's own first, and then expanding that loyalty to include more and more people, should be expressed in the family by loyalty to one's spouse first, even before one's children.

A father I know had just told his daughter that she couldn't have any more cookies from a tray. Just then the mother came onto the scene. "Mommy," the little girl cried through wheedling tears, "Daddy won't let me have any more cookies!" "Well," said the mother conciliatingly, "you may have just one more." One more! She might as well have given her the whole tray. Already the lesson had been conveyed: "Don't listen to Daddy any more. Listen to me."

Parents must back one another up. Even if you think your wife or husband is mistaken, you cannot afford to present a divided front to your children.

Of course, I am referring here to situations where discipline is involved. If instead the husband says that Venus is in the evening sky, and the wife happens to know that it is Mercury, what is the harm of pointing out the error? By a parental example of

harmonious disagreement the children may
even receive a valuable lesson in how to
handle similar situations in their own lives.

But when it comes to disciplining them,
remember that, however ignorant they may be
in other departments, when it comes to
politics they are masters! Somehow they
understand the art from the very cradle. They
know absolutely how to divide and conquer.
And even before they have learned to speak,
they know how to play upon your emotions to
get what they want. So keep that front united!
Be true and loyal first to each other.

Another very important point with
children is to be absolutely fair with them.
Never speak to them from a feeling of anger.

That isn't always easy! I remember once
when we were staying with relatives. Dad was
dressed in his Sunday best, eating breakfast
before going to church. Little Eddie, my
somewhat smart-aleck cousin, was sitting next
to him. Suddenly Eddie's voice piped up,
"Uncle Ray, I'm spreading oatmeal on your
coat." And he was, too, in thick layers. Dad's
annoyance was, I think, fairly understandable.
It was probably the only response Eddie
would have understood at that time.

Let's face it, children can sometimes
drive you batty! In fact, sometimes it is their

whole intention to do so. But remember that if you respond to them in kind, usually you'll lose your hold on them. They test you to see if they can pull you down to their level of immaturity. But if even once they succeed, they may never again give you full the respect due to an adult.

Always, therefore, speak to them from a sense of justice. Be fair. Be impartial. In this way you may scold them even severely—and sometimes you may need to; you can't always be shining through with sweetness and light—and still you'll have their respect.

If, furthermore, you speak to them even scoldingly, but with love, you'll still have their love.

Sometimes my guru had to shout at us, his adult children, to get a message to sink through our thick skulls.

A little boy runs out into a street, busy with traffic. How are you going to handle the situation? Will you call to him sweetly, "Come back, Johnny. You might get run over"? Certainly not! You'll grab him by the scruff of the neck, perhaps give him a good wallop to make sure you impress it on him never to do such a thing again, even shout at him to make very sure he gets the message once and forever.

Adults aren't used to being spoken to in this way. Once one realizes, however, that full maturity isn't something one attains at eighteen or twenty-one, that it means wisdom and the perfection of all soul-qualities, and that an arduous and long apprenticeship is necessary if one is to attain such a state, one gladly embraces such discipline as one requires to grow spiritually.

Life itself contrives to teach us many lessons the hard way. Scolding from a wise guru may impress on a disciple the need for changing a course of behavior which otherwise might bring the disciple great suffering. Considered as an alternative to that suffering, the guru's scolding—like that of the parent whose child runs out into traffic—is a demonstration of pure love. And that is what I saw in my guru's eyes on the few occasions when he scolded me. I saw regret, deep concern for my welfare, and unconditional love.

Sometimes, then, to make a point, you may have to resort to strong discipline. But if you do so, never, never speak or act with personal feeling. If you do, he'll be able to feel your emotion. And he'll remember it long afterwards as a time when you allowed a fleeting situation to take precedence over your love for him. Such memories can be traumatic in the lives of adults as well as of children.

A related point to the above is this one: Never, in any loving relationship, allow the people involved to assume secondary importance, in your eyes, to the outward circumstances of your relationship.

People are more important than things.

Should you every spank your child? Many parents are so opposed to the practice that they will wax angry if the question is merely raised. But I think we have to take into account the different personalities of children.

Some children are more identified with their bodies than others are. They may sometimes, therefore, need their lessons administered in a physical manner if they are going to heed them at all. But other children live more in their minds. To them, a lesson administered physically may seem a great indignity.

In my own family as I grew up, I was the thinker; my brother Bob, the doer. If ever Bob was spanked, he would forget about it almost immediately; there was no trauma involved. Sometimes it was the best way of getting through to him. But if ever I was spanked, which fortunately was seldom, I never forgot it. I remember once looking at my father weeks after a spanking, and demanding accusingly, "Why did you spank me?" It had been the wrong way to get through to me.

In fairness to my father, however, I should add that he was always scrupulously just. It was above all his sense of fairness and justice that impressed his lessons on our minds. Fairness and justice are, I believe, what all children respect. Parents who fly off the handle simply to release their own emotions end up not being listened to at all by their children. "Oh, there's old Dad, blowing off again!" You will only win your children's respect if you make justice the basis of your discipline—particularly if the justice is directed toward what is right and best for them.

Above all, they will respect and love you if you temper justice with compassion. Let them know you are their friend. They'll respond more to love even than to justice. We all need mercy occasionally. Let them know that you are on their side—that you are their true friend.

It is important also, however, to let them know that you won't stand for any nonsense. You have to be firm. You see, children are always trying to find out where their limits are; and if you keep backing off because of blind love for them, they'll be spoiled. And what does it mean to be spoiled? It means to grow up with the thought that, somehow —if necessary by throwing a tantrum—one can always get his way. It means to be spoiled for objective reality, by always living a dream. It means being unable to relate to anyone's realities but one's own—a constricted world to live in indeed! Such an attitude is the very opposite of self-expansion. And it is the surest road to future unhappiness as an adult.

Children need the sense of security that comes from knowing what their limits are. They need to feel that, within a given mental enclosure, the territory is unassailably theirs. But from that sure base they also need to be allowed—indeed, encouraged—to expand. The trick is not to impose expansion on them, but to encourage them to seek it for themselves. The trick also is not to impose your own limitations on them (the parents, for instance, who don't want their musically gifted child to practice the piano because the sound bothers them). If you keep their limits unnaturally narrow you will suffocate their growth.

It is important, then, to develop a feeling for each child's potentials, but within the limits of those potentials to try sensitively to wean him to an acceptance of ever broader horizons.

If you are truly a loving parent, this will mean also weaning him gradually from dependence on home and family. For sooner or later he will have to go out anyway and face the world alone. The time to prepare him for independence is now.

Let him mix more with his peers. At Ananda Village we let those children who so desire live through the week in a dormitory with others of their own sex. The choice to live in the dormitory is up to them; we don't force the issue. But if they themselves feel ready, they may live several days a week with their peers under the supervision of an adult. In this way they develop responsibility and independence, and are gradually prepared for the day when they will be on their own.

Children need security, but to give them too much security is not good for them. To give them too much money, for example, might spoil them. This will be true even after they grow up. Yogananda said that wealthy people who leave all their money to their children make a great mistake—at least until such a time as those "children" become mature adults, and successful in their own right. Parents who can afford to do so should give their offspring enough money to get started in life, and to stand on their own feet, but not enough to encourage lasting dependence. They may not thank you in the beginning, but they'll be sure to thank you later.

Try also to put them on their own feet emotionally as soon as possible. How soon? A friend of mine, who returned from India recently, reported an interesting observation that she and the group she'd gone with had made. They had been astonished never to see a crying child. That is to say, as soon as a child began crying, its mother would lift it up in her lap and cuddle it. And the sense of security this attention induced in the child seemed to keep it emotionally serene. Here in America it may be that we try to wean them from that security too soon.

So when I speak of weaning them emotionally, I mean to wean them at their own natural pace, with sensitivity to *their* rhythms. Some children should be weaned sooner. Others, more psychologically dependent, may need to be weaned more slowly. Take the child's individuality into account.

As a general rule, I would say that the first six years are years of total dependence, and the next six of only slowly diminishing dependence. By the time a child reaches his teens, normally, is the time to encourage him to discipline himself more and more to stand on his own.

Above all, try always to direct the development of your children toward an expanding view of the true meaning of family—not the "us four and no more" consciousness, but an acceptance of all mankind as their broader family.

CHAPTER 7

Religion & Family Life

Suppose you want to spiritualize your marriage and family life, according to the precepts in this book, but your spouse doesn't. Is there anything you can do?

Or suppose both of you are spiritually inclined, but your children aren't. Is there any way you can win them to spiritual attitudes without seeming to force them?

How far should you go, in any case, in offering them spiritual teachings? Would *any* effort in this direction constitute an impingement on their free will?

And how far should you compromise your ideals with an unsympathetic mate? Should your marriage take precedence over every other consideration, even the spiritual?

I mentioned earlier that, spiritually speaking, a marriage may be said not even to be consummated until at least some degree of spiritual union has been achieved. Does this mean that spiritual incompatibility might, in a court of spiritual law, be fair grounds for annulment?

These are all difficult questions— difficult primarily because individual cases will require individual consideration. But certain universal principles are involved also; these at least can be touched on here.

The first of these principles is free will. It would be going against this principle to try to coerce *anyone*, even your nearest and dearest, into embracing your ideals. In connection with this principle, however, it should be understood that there need be nothing coercive about sharing one's enthusiasms, nor about inviting people to consider one's beliefs, so long as they themselves are open to such sharing.

The second principle is that self-expansion is the essence of every meaningful relationship. Where inner growth ceases, stagnation sets in. Even stagnation, moreover, psychologically speaking, is not a static condition; always it involves a sense of contraction, a shrinking inward upon the ego. Where compromise is concerned, therefore, if that compromise is based expansively on sympathy for one's mate, or on tolerance for his (or for her) realities, something of spiritual value may be found even in a relationship in which one's own spouse doesn't share one's dearest ideals. But if the compromise is of the ideals themselves, the decision to accept such a compromise may only kill everything that makes your relationship worthwhile.

The third principle is a guideline for right living that is offered by the Indian Scriptures: "Where a duty conflicts with a higher duty, it ceases to be a duty."

Certainly, the ideal relationship in a spiritual marriage would be where both husband and wife love God, and seek Him together. It is the happiest arrangement also when both follow the same spiritual path, and can share the same practices and beliefs. A spiritually compatible couple, moreover, will be more likely to attract spiritual souls as their children. Happy indeed is the family in which parents and children meditate together, serve

God together, and share the highest goal to which men or angels can aspire: union with God.

But life doesn't always smoothe our path out before us so pleasantly. And perhaps it is just as well that it does not. We don't grow without obstacles, and those obstacles are seldom those we would have chosen for ourselves! Perhaps your husband is unsympathetic to your spiritual efforts. Should you leave him? Is there a chance that you might win him over? And if so, how? Remember, I said at the outset that individual cases need individual handling. All I can offer here are very general guidelines. It all comes back, in the last analysis, to where *you* are.

There is a law of magnetism (you might even list this among the others above as a fourth principle, though I prefer for the continuity of thought to keep it here): *A strong human magnet will influence a weaker one—for good or for evil, according to the quality of its own magnetism.* A strongly spiritual person, in other words, will exert an uplifting influence on a weaker, though basically materialistic person, and has nothing to fear spiritually from him even in the close association of matrimony. But if one is spiritually weak, and is married to someone who is strongly materialistic, he has everything to fear, spiritually, from their association.

A further factor might be considered: namely, that *any* effort positively directed will generate more magnetic power, usually, than efforts directed toward merely blocking such effort. In other words, if your spouse's resistance to your spiritual efforts is based only on an effort to keep you in your accustomed rut, the chances are that even if you consider your magnetism weaker than his (or than hers), the very fact that you are making an effort to grow may render you immune, at least in this matter, to his influence.

Marriage is a sacred bond only if it is made sacred. Otherwise it is a social contract, one to be taken seriously, certainly, but not placed above every other possible consideration. If you can remain married to an unspiritually inclined mate even though your own feet are planted firmly on the path, there may be important spiritual lessons for you to learn from this relationship. Even if your mate seems to obstruct your spiritual efforts, you may gain greatly in inner strength if you generate the inner strength to meet that obstruction. Remember Yogananda's words: "There are no such things as obstacles; there are only opportunities!" Moreover, there may be the possibility that, by your quiet example, your mate may gradually be won to a more spiritual way of life.

Only if your marriage really threatens your spiritual development should you seriously contemplate divorce. Under such circumstances, your highest duty must be seen to be your duty to God.

There is nothing wrong in trying to share your own highest interests and ideals with others, particularly with those whom you love. But sharing is one thing, and proselytizing another. Don't try to drive your beliefs down their throats: You'll only end up antagonizing them. I made this mistake with people when I was new on the path; I know, therefore, what I'm talking about! It didn't work.

Attract them by your own increased joy and calmness. But *let them come to you.* Try to project your spiritual influence in such a way that it works on them like leaven—from within—rather than from without, through a barrage of mere words and Wholesome Thoughts.

Be firm in your own spiritual principles and practices, but don't put out, even mentally, the suggestion that this is something they should be doing also. Respect their freedom to follow their own way, to take whatever detours they need to take in order to learn their own lessons in life. Remember, there are many, many grades in this cosmic school of spiritual education.

With your children, as I have already implied, don't hesitate to share with them your spiritual ideals, so long as they are open to this kind of influence. I don't at all go along with the popular argument that children shouldn't be taught religion for fear of imposing on their free will. As well might one claim that they shouldn't be taught anything at all!

But at the same time it is important to remember that they have come into their present bodies trailing all sorts of clouds behind them, and not always (to again quote Wordsworth) clouds of glory. They have their own destinies to work out; in no way are they mere blank slates at birth. You may have one child that is naturally spiritual, and another that simply is not. In this case, give spiritual energy openly to the one who is receptive to it, but perhaps only in prayer to the one who is not.

Your duty as a parent is in any case not absolute. You and your spouse were vehicles, simply, through which they entered this world to pursue their own soul-evolution.

But can you, in this case, attract spiritual souls to your family? Yes, you can. Souls are attracted to parents according to certain natural affinities that they feel for them. Peaceful parents are more likely than excitable ones to attract souls with a love of peace. Noble-minded parents are more likely to attract similarly inclined children. I say "*more* likely" because such is the complexity of human nature that compatibility in one trait is no guarantee of equal compatibility in all. Peace-loving and noble-minded parents, for example, may attract a child that is equally peace-loving, but not particularly noble-minded. Still, the more you project, during conception, thoughts of the kind of child you want to attract, the greater the likelihood that that is the sort of soul that will be drawn to your family—just as, if you extend a graciously worded invitation to your house to dinner, a sensitive person will be more likely to accept, even if his original intentions were to go elsewhere that evening.

Conception, Yogananda said, is the moment at which the soul enters the womb. He described it as a flash of light in the astral world, to which souls with an affinity for that particular light (assuming they've reached the point where they are ready for physical birth) are attracted. When you and your spouse come together to conceive a child, therefore, mentally send out an invitation to the kind of child you would like to welcome into your home. Still better, if both of you are on the spiritual path, spend several months before this important occasion, meditating, and lovingly inviting a spiritual soul to be born to you.

The mental and spiritual influence of the parents, and especially of the mother, on the developing embryo is a further, and vitally important, consideration. The mother especially should make every effort to keep herself free from moods, and to project wholesome thoughts to the being whose body is growing within her. In my own case, my mother kept praying throughout her pregnancy, "This first child I give to God." And that thought has been perhaps the single most powerful direction in my life.

If you and your spouse can have a room that you set aside for meditation, all the better. Meditate some time together every day. But give each other the freedom also to meditate alone. Although it is beautiful to grow spiritually together, room should remain for the realization that your search for God is, in the last analysis, an inward one, and one that you must in the end, pursue alone.

If your children want to meditate with you, encourage them to do so, but preferably at a time when you can accommodate yourself comfortably to a very much shortened session. Don't, if you can help it, sacrifice too much of your own precious time with God.

Finally, if you feel that the influence in your home is not sufficiently conducive to your own spiritual growth, you needn't therefore renounce your family. Instead, you might attend spiritual gatherings elsewhere, or invite spiritually inclined friends to your home at times when their presence will not interfere with the normal activities of your spouse and children. Under all circumstances remember this dictum: Wherever God places you, there He must come.

CHAPTER 8

Questions & Answers

This book is based on material taken from a class that I gave at Ananda Meditation Retreat. At the end of that class I invited questions from the audience. A number of these questions are appended here.

Question. Should one be completely honest with one's spouse?

Answer. I don't recommend it! In most cases, of course, yes. But you're dealing here with someone of only relative wisdom. Your spouse, like you, probably labors under his own share of delusions. Under such circumstances, I think there are bound to be certain things that are simply best left unsaid.

For example, let us say that it bothers you that your wife combs her hair on the left side instead of in the middle. Trivial, obviously. But if there's any danger that it might hurt her for you to say so, why not remain silent? Again, to tell her frankly that you consider her hat ugly, when you know she had her heart set on buying it—I don't think that kind of honesty is helpful. This, then, first of all, ought to be one's guideline: to speak the *beneficial* truth. Truth, my guru said, is *always* beneficial.

This raises a further, and important, consideration: A difference sometimes exists between truth and mere fact. To tell a person that he looks ill may be to state a fact, but it may also make him feel twice as badly as before! Is it a truth? No, for in his deepest reality—the soul—he can never be ill.

On the other hand, to tell him he looks great may be overstating the case. But why not speak encouragingly? Why not say, for instance, if there's any chance of meaning it, "You look better today"? Such an affirmative statement may give him the courage he needs to become well.

A saint may actually tell a sick man, "You are well!" and say it with such conviction that he actually cures him. The saint's vision, you see, penetrates the material veil. He can see through the delusion of illness to the reality of the soul, which is ever perfect.

Out of sheer respect for other people's right to work out their delusions at their own speed, it is necessary at times to use discrimination in the degree of your openness with them.

There is another aspect to the matter, too. In moments of confidence we sometimes tell people things which they later hold over us—perhaps in moments when they are angry or upset with us. Their negative thoughts about us may act upon us mesmerically, making it all the more difficult for us to change even if we sincerely want to.

None of this is to say that we should not be honest with others, and particularly with those whom we love. Honesty and truthfulness are two of the most important qualities for spiritual advancement. But honesty with others should be tempered by common sense. Confession and frankness are always best directed where they will be rightly understood, and not misused: if possible to the wise, and *always*, in one's heart, to God. From God not even the flicker of a thought should be hidden.

In conclusion, remember that love, often, is the highest honesty. It contains more truth by far than brutal frankness, by which one's deepest feelings are often obscured.

Question. Is it ever good to be self-assertive in our relationship with our friends, our spouse, or our children?

Answer. Within reason, I think so. If you try to "do right by" others at the *expense* of your own happiness, you'll be unfair to yourself, and won't really be helping them. But the other side of the picture is that, for a person on the spiritual path, to learn to live for other people can be a great gain.

Someone who has taken an "assertive-ness training" seminar may tell such a spiritually inclined person, "Listen, you never say what you want." "But I don't want *anything*," replies the devotee. "But you *have* to want *something!*" objects the assertiveness trainee. "Well, I just don't." Worldly people can't understand such an attitude. Their whole lives revolve around "getting theirs." But the devotee understands.

A person should try, if he wants to live a spiritual life, to bring himself to the point where he is able completely to accept whatever happens. He knows that only from a point of such acceptance—that is to say, from relating to the reality of a situation, and not to his mere wishes regarding it—can he hope to make any changes that may need to be made. But you must also be honest with yourself about your own present realities. If you'd *like* to accept a situation, but in fact can't accept it at all, why try to squelch your impulse to reject it? Your rejection will only come out in some other, and probably much less wholesome, manner.

Sometimes in a relationship it is necessary to stand up for yourself. This doesn't mean you have to bite the other person! But sometimes it may be necessary to bark. You have to protect your own peace of mind. You have to protect your privacy. It's necessary for you to decide what you're to do. You can't be forever depriving yourself with a view to doing what others want of you. Moreover, you'll gain nothing, even spiritually, if you allow yourself to be a doormat for others.

Don't allow others to impose on you endlessly. Do things because you inwardly decide to do them, rather than because someone else is dragging you into them. If you allow yourself to be dragged, eventually you'll

become just a sort of human puppy dog.
You'll lose your sense of self-worth. So in that
way, you see, self-assertiveness is essential. It
becomes wrong when you try to assert your
desires over the desires of others, and to
impose your wishes on them.

Question. In Paramhansa Yogananda's
"Vows at Marriage" there is the statement,
"May our children serve as spiritual ushers to
bring others back from delusion's home."
What if a couple don't want to have children?

Answer. Well, obviously, not everyone
who marries is going to have children. Some
may be too old. Some may not be able to have
them. Still others may simply not want them. I
would say that for those on the spiritual path
who don't want children, and who would
rather devote their energies to meditation and
to otherwise serving God, it would be placing
an intolerable burden on them to insist that
they *must* produce offspring. What for—if
they don't want it? It wouldn't be fair even to
the child to bring him into the family under
such circumstances.

I think the idea is that if you do have
children, then may they serve as spiritual
ushers. But it can't mean that you *must* have
children in order to create more spiritual
ushers!

Question. If one is single, but wants to be married, how can he attract a spiritual mate?

Answer. I find that a great deal of energy is wasted in wondering, "When am I going to meet my soul mate?" For someone who is on the spiritual path, it is wisest to seek God first of all, deeply. The Lord will send the right person to you—in His own time. Through your meditation and devotion you will develop the magnetism to attract such a person.

Perhaps the most helpful words in the Bible in this regard are the promise of Jesus: "Seek the kingdom of God first, and all these things shall be added unto you" (Matthew 6:33). Develop spiritual magnetism through daily communion with Him, and you'll draw true friends to you—those who are compatible with you on the highest, soul level.

Question. You mentioned the "dry spells" that occur in marriage, as also on the spiritual path. How may one know if the indifference he feels is just a temporary "dry spell," or a sign that he should end the marriage?

Answer. Well, on the spiritual path the wise seeker certainly doesn't draw the conclusion from a dry spell, no matter how long its duration, that it is time he got divorced from God! ("Goodbye God and all your crazy crowd! I'm going back to city life and good times.") We can't escape God anyway. We are forever a part of Him. However long it takes us, our only hope of permanent release from suffering is to attain union with Him.

The case of marriage is more similar than it may at first seem. For though we may divorce our wife or husband, we can't obtain a divorce from ourselves! And usually it is from within ourselves that our troubles spring.

I often tell the story of a monk in the monastery I lived in in Los Angeles who left, partly because there was another monk living there whom he simply couldn't stand. On a visit to us a year later, he confessed ruefully, "Do you remember how I hated J——? Well, where I'm working now there are six others exactly like him!"

When we try to escape our problems, you see, they tend only to grow in size—which is another way of saying that *we* shrink in our ability to handle them. It is a statistical fact that people who get divorced are more likely to get divorced a second, or a third time. Only if they learn from their first (or second) experience, and make an effort to change themselves, are their chances better of marrying successfully the next time.

Is divorce ever right? I think so. Especially if a relationship becomes spiritually stagnant. In such circumstances, one may safely conclude that those lessons have now been learned which that relationship was intended to provide. Continued growth, even through the painful avenue of divorce, is forever our highest duty.

But divorce, at the same time, is by no means a step to be taken lightly. Every effort should be made to salvage a marriage before it is finally abandoned. Even stagnation, after all, may be only temporary, or only apparent. Dry spells on the spiritual path, too, seem like stagnation, but if one keeps plodding steadily onward he finds eventually that in fact he was working out certain obstacles in himself. Once those problems are worked out, all the accustomed sweetness will return.

In marriage, as in life, it is wise to develop long rhythms. Don't leap to hasty conclusions. Wait out today's dryness. Tomorrow, or next week, or next month, the drought may end, perhaps forever. I remember a dry spell in my own meditations that lasted a year and a half. But how thankful I am that I never sought the solution of leaving my meditative practices!

Because human feelings fluctuate, I think, as I said earlier, that the surest bond in marriage is not love, but respect. Love flourishes when it is rooted in respect. I spoke earlier, also, of the false expectations with which people approach marriage. They expect a lifetime of candles and roses. When that first romantic bloom fades, they suppose that love itself has died. Obviously, this is a false expectation.

It is perfectly normal for romantic love to develop into more of a friendly relationship. Couples who don't make unreasonable demands of each other are much more likely to remain married than those incurable romantics who, because of their addiction to matrimony, may be looked to by their friends as offering the greatest promise of happiness in their marriages.

Question. If one person comes onto the spiritual path, but her spouse doesn't, how is she to convey to him that she feels differently now about having sex all the time, and that it would mean more to both of them if they reserved it for special occasions?

Answer. I must say, I admire your courage in asking such a question! Many, I suspect, have held the question in their hearts, but never dared asked it. So let me try to answer for their sakes, too. But mind you, I'll have to go out on a limb myself now. I know of no scriptural authority for what I am about to tell you.

I suggest you look upon your husband as a child in this matter—as one who needs to be raised gradually to a more mature understanding. *You've* understood that there's a higher way to live, but he hasn't understood it yet. Now, supposing after your visit to Ananda you go back enthusiastically and say to him, "Honey, let's practice self-control." What effect will your words have? Probably he'll define the entire spiritual path in terms of the threat it poses to his sex life! Why not try, rather, to deal with the matter in a way that he can accept? Win him by positive, not by negative, means.

Emphasize those aspects of the path that he is more likely to appreciate. Show him benefits he can relate to—your increased calmness, perhaps, or your greater capacity for joy; or, best of all, your deepened love for him. He'll start talking about this philosophy as something that makes people happier. Only after he sees and accepts the positive side would it be wise to say, "Honey, you know one thing that would make us even happier? . . ." Wait till you can get through to him. I don't know what the saints would

say to this, but I think we must keep our
philosophy practical.

Question. Because of the emotional tie
that exists between married people, they are
much more sensitive to one another's moods
and feelings than to those of most people.
How can I remain calm when my spouse is
upset?

Answer. There are two factors at work
here. First is the influence itself; but second is
the belief that it would show a lack of proper
support *not* to be influenced. I can address the
second more easily than the first.

The point is that we don't help anyone by
getting sympathetically upset just because he
is upset. (Do you help a drowning man by
jumping into the water and drowning with
him?) You may show sympathy, yes. It
certainly wouldn't help matters, if your wife is
upset about something, to make it absolutely
clear to her (and to all the neighbors) how
very calm *you* are about it all. ("It's your
problem, dear. Ha ha! Look at me. *I* don't let
trifles like that bother me!")

One-upsmanship is the last game one
ought to play at such times. Unfortunately,
for many people it is the first—their golden
opportunity to advertise their own sterling

qualities. But a sensitive person will set himself aside when his spouse is upset. Surely he will show sympathy, if only by respectful silence. But there is a difference between sympathy and pity.

To pity someone means to enter into his suffering. Pity weakens the resolution of the sufferer to get out of his suffering. It only reinforces the pain.

Do you owe it to your spouse to get upset when she (or when he) is upset? Certainly not! Rather, you owe it to her *not* to get upset. Support her, not in her mood, but in her unhappiness with the mood, in her wish for harmony. If on the other hand she is upset with some objective circumstance, but you feel she is wrong, or perhaps over-reacting, silently give her love. Don't jeer at her even mentally for her mistake. (We all make them, don't we?) Give her mental support—not for her mood, but for what she means to you in spite of her mood.

The first thing people usually demand when they are upset is that others agree with them. If there is any ground on which you *can* agree, without becoming upset yourself, it may help matters for you to go along with some of your spouse's negative feelings. But try to bring calmness to the scene as soon as

comfortably possible, for it is only from a
center of calmness that the best energy can
ensue—even to right a definite wrong.

But love is the best guide in such
circumstances. I may make suggestions, but if
you love your spouse your heart will dictate
the appropriate response in a greater variety of
situations than I can possibly visualize here. In
any case, what I personally find most helpful
of all when dealing with people who are upset
is not some mentally prepared list of
appropriate responses, but a sort of
withdrawal into myself in a search for
superconscious guidance on how to handle
the matter.

This withdrawal into the inner Self is
important also as a protection against being
influenced by the other's mood. With
someone as close as one's own spouse, such an
influence is a powerful factor, and one that
will have to be dealt with.

It may help, as a means of self-protection,
to go off by yourself for a while. Take a walk.
Go to your room and meditate. Or go
outdoors and do some deep breathing. Get
calm first, then come back and see what you
can do to improve matters. If you try to be
helpful while you yourself are upset, you will
only succeed in adding fuel to the fire.

Question. You speak of giving respect. How can respect be simply given—freely, as it were? Isn't it something that must be earned?

Answer. I see your point, but forgive me if I disagree with you—respectfully, of course! What I've observed in life is that those who are the least qualified—by skill, training, or position—are usually the least apt to show respect to others; while those with the highest qualifications are often quite humble about them, and respectful to everyone.

The ability to feel respect, you see, is a mark of refinement. To become highly qualified in one's own field often requires a certain refinement also. That is why the highest achievements and an attitude of humble respectfulness to all so often go hand in hand.

Paramhansa Yogananda, in referring to the great horticulturist Luther Burbank, commented, "The modesty with which he wore his scientific fame repeatedly reminded me of the trees that bend low with the burden of ripening fruits; it is the barren tree that lifts its head high in an empty boast."*

---

*Paramhansa Yogananda, *Autobiography of a Yogi*, Los Angeles, Self-Realization Publishers, 1971, p. 366.

Yogananda himself was the most respectful human being I ever met. One would have thought that a person of his attainments didn't owe it to *anyone* to show respect. Yet he gave it to the veriest fool.

Respect, in other words, is something we should learn to give freely. We should not have to wait until it is dragged grudgingly from us.

And we give it naturally, unstintingly, if in our hearts we have learned to respect ourselves.

CHAPTER 9
*An Interview**

S*cience* of Mind: *You have said that marriage should be based on spiritual principles. How can that be done and what value does it have?*

Swami Kriyananda: "From a spiritual viewpoint, marriage is seen to be a vehicle by which the soul achieves union with God.

*An interview with Swami Kriyananda by Ronald S. Miller. Science of Mind Magazine, April 1984. © Science of Mind 1984. Reprinted with permission.

Because this union transcends any purely physical or institutional consideration, marriage must be honored first and foremost as a spiritual condition, a training ground to prepare people for the higher union. Thus the ultimate purpose of marriage is to bring us out of ourselves, out of the narrow confines of selfishness and ego, so we may begin to live a more sanctified life, dedicated to a reality larger than our own.

"Nobody is married spiritually if he is married to his partner only on a mundane level. Thus Indian scriptures say that husband and wife shouldn't love each other only for the sake of each other, but for the sake of God, whom they see in one another. Unless marriage is spiritualized, it cannot be successful in the deepest sense, because the very basis of true marriage is a love that is spiritual, not earthly."

So the outer, physical marriage should indicate that a marriage has also taken place on a deeper level within the psyches of the two partners.

Kriyananda: "Yes. Besides being a path to Divine union, marriage is also a way for men and women to balance their natures, since we are instinctively drawn to the opposite sex for reasons that transcend mere sexual attraction. Men and women generally need to balance their somewhat one-sided natures, and they unconsciously seek the opposite sex to a-chieve a state of psychic wholeness.

"Men, for example, generally express more reason, while their feeling nature is kept hidden and undeveloped. Conversely, women usually express more feeling, while the reason-ing nature is more hidden. This doesn't mean that men have no capacity for love or women have no capacity for reason. It's just that men tend to depend more on reason and women tend to depend more on feeling.

"Most of us find it advantageous to be closely affiliated with somebody who has qualities which are complementary to our own nature. So, in marriage, we enter into deep communion with our opposite, com-plementary quality, which therefore no longer remains buried in our own unconscious. We learn, in effect, to balance feeling and reason. Actually, this balance already exists within us in our relationship to God, though we're usually not aware of it. So the inner union which takes place in us as a result of marriage prepares the way for us eventually to become aware of that Divine balance."

You're saying that when a person is deeply committed to spiritual realization, marriage not

*only doesn't interfere with that commitment, but
can actually contribute to its depth.*

Kriyananda: "Yes, although for us to
understand this idea, we need to view marriage in a new light. Over the centuries, in the
East as well as in the West, the notion grew
that monastic withdrawal from the distrac-
tions of daily life was the preferred path to
God. Without the emotional attachments that
marriage brings, one could wholeheartedly
concentrate his energies on pursuing the
higher life. But it seems incompatible with the
way the Spirit is moving in modern life for
people to retreat into a desert to find God.
The time has come, I believe, to work toward
greater unity, and toward resolving differences — to proclaim the basic oneness of the
world's religions, for example, and to show
that the path to God depends not on specific
outward patterns of living, but on inward
commitment. Old, unilinear concepts need to
be broadened.

"In speaking of marriage versus renunciation in an early edition of *Autobiography of a
Yogi,* my spiritual teacher, Paramhansa Yogananda, said, 'To fulfill one's earthly responsi-
bilities is indeed the higher path, provided the
yogi, maintaining a mental uninvolvement
with egotistical desires, plays his part as a

willing instrument of God.' In other words, if a person can live *in* the world without being *of* it, the inner strength he gains in consequence will actually aid his spiritual efforts."

But how can this ideal be achieved on a practical level?

Kriyananda: "At Ananda Cooperative Village, where I live with several hundred other spiritual seekers, we have synthesized the 'renunciate' path, with its emphasis on living for God alone, with the 'householder' path, with its unique opportunity for testing spiritual values on the human plane. The result is what we call *renunciate marriage*, an ideal which embodies self-offering rather than self-rejection.

"Renunciation, whether in a cave or in the home, is basically the surrendering of self and self-will, with the view of following God's will, rather than the path of one's personal desire. At Ananda our couples are devoted to serving God's will *first*, even if it seems to conflict with their personal preferences. What we have found is that those couples who place God first, as their highest priority, find harmony flowing into every other aspect of life. However, those who place marriage above the demands of the Divine will also frequently experience disharmony and disruption in their marriages.

"If marriage is based on the ideal of renunciation — renunciation of self-will, desire, and attachment — then it can hardly be seen as interfering with the depth of one's spiritual commitment. Admittedly, it's hard to live a married life without falling prey to attachments of various kinds; it's harder to live only for God when you have somebody to support, but it is possible. But because the varying demands of householder life are more difficult than the monastic approach, its rewards may in fact be greater. My true inclination, however, is not to elevate one path over the other, but merely to indicate that whatever path through life one chooses, *renunciation of personal desire is always the essence of spiritual growth.*"

As desire is purified through spiritualized marriage, the initial physical attraction which drew a couple together would evolve into a higher, more refined love. So if a couple used their relationship as a vehicle to seek and to serve God, how would that evolution take place over the years?

Kriyananda: "Slowly, over time, the couple would internalize their relationship, placing more and more emphasis on the subtle, inner connection rather than on the outward, physical one. In other words, in their closeness the partners would literally carry each other within themselves, regardless of their physical proximity. They would be content being quiet together, without the need for constant verbal stimulation. They would know each other's thoughts without being the least bit intrusive."

Wouldn't this kind of inner contentment make certain practices — like meditation — easier?

Kriyananda: "This is quite true. Spiritual marriage reduces the mind's restlessness and allows one to focus his gaze inward, where he can draw undistractedly from the wellspring of his own being. The outer contentment one experiences with his partner should in all circumstances lead to an ever-increasing inwardness, even in sexual union itself. In this most intimate aspect of marital life, one can cultivate the attitude that he's not reaching outward for joy, but is reaching inward for communion with the higher Self, where alone perfect union is found. A time will eventually come when inner communion becomes constant over the years, and need no longer be affirmed outwardly through sexual union."

How does "ordinary marriage" — the traditional romantic model subscribed to by our culture — differ from the ideal marriage you've just described?

Kriyananda: "The basic difference between an ordinary and a spiritual marriage is whether one is living for himself or for Truth. In its highest sense, marriage is a path to expand one's identity ever outward — from a limited sense of ego-identity to one's spouse, from spouse to children, then from family to neighbors, countrymen, all mankind, and to the very ocean of life which surrounds and nourishes us. Anything which helps us break out of the confines of selfishness will benefit us. Often, in ordinary marriage, those confines are merely affirmed and strengthened. The husband, for example, to support *his* wife and *his* family, may show a lack of sensitivity for the needs of others that he'd never show if he were acting only for himself. In this way, marital commitment is often used to excuse behavior that is contrary to all spiritual law — in ignorance of the truth which is articulated in Indian scriptures: 'If a duty conflicts with a higher duty or principle, it ceases to be a duty.'

"For spiritual people, marriage represents an expansion of the ego; for worldly people, it represents a reinforcement and

contraction of the ego into a limited and cozy
state of self-enclosure, rather than a window
onto ever-greater realities. In a worldly marriage people seek to gain from each other. But
in a spiritual marriage people seek to gain *for*
each other, and to give to each other. Worldly
marriage partners ask, 'What can I derive
from this relationship?' Spiritual partners
constantly seek ways to give *to* their relationship.

"In an ordinary marriage, if the husband
is floundering in his spiritual dedication and
the wife is not supportive of his overall
efforts, she might encourage him to give up his
attempts and return to his former habits of
living. In effect, she would be pampering his
ego rather than reinforcing his soul aspiration.
In a higher marriage, if one partner feels weak,
the other doesn't pander to that weakness, but
tries ever to draw out the spouse's highest
potential, even when the spouse feels out of
touch with his own true depths."

*In an ordinary marriage, then, the partners
might cling to each other through fear and
dependency. But to a spiritual couple, the marriage can be a form of spiritual discipline used to
purify the ego through close daily contact.*

Kriyananda: "This is definitely true. It's
so easy to be considerate, polite, and kind to a

stranger to whom your kindness doesn't entail
a commitment because you won't see him
again. It's easy then, isn't it, to rise to heroic
heights of kindness and courtesy! But to live
with somebody at close quarters and to
demonstrate that same considerateness requires great self-discipline and is the real test
of how one is developing spiritually.

"In other words, we have to submit our
spiritual progress to the trials of daily life. As
one saint put it, 'Your religion is tested in the
cold light of day.' If you feel peace in
meditation but that peace is rattled as soon as
somebody spills coffee on your tie, then the
peace you experienced in meditation has yet
to be made real on that other level of your life.
In an intimate relationship like marriage, if
you can still affirm peace, love, and forgive-
ness through the ups and downs of daily life,
your spiritual progress is assured.

"Actually, a steadfast commitment to
one person draws out the spiritual potential
which might otherwise remain hidden if the
friction of daily contact were removed. Once,
a Catholic saint, St. Therese of Lisieux, was
speaking to someone about several embittered
nuns, who, presumably, had lost their voca-
tion and didn't have the courage to leave the
monastery. These women would intentionally

wash clothes, for example, so vigorously that the soap suds would splatter in other people's eyes. When Therese was asked why such people were to be found in a house of God, she replied, 'If we didn't have them, it would behoove us to go out and find them and bring them here, because people like that help us grow.'

"If everyone treated us peacefully, how would we ever know when we'd reached that level of true peace which can withstand all tests? We have to clarify our discrimination through the strains imposed on us in our close relationships. The only caveat is that we should use the discrimination we develop to be supportive, never to be critical."

One of the main tenets of spiritual life is not to judge others. Yet as we observe our partner's weaknesses, how can we help that partner change without being critical and judgmental?

Kriyananda: "The main thing is to work on changing yourself and to realize that you are not your brother's or even your partner's keeper. In the truest spiritual sense, we must give all people the freedom to evolve in their own way. This doesn't mean blinding ourselves to our partner's weaknesses, but it does mean wedding our powers of discernment to genuine kindness when we discuss those weaknesses.

"The scriptural commandment not to judge others refers to *disliking* them for their flaws and is not a warning against developing the soul-faculty of discrimination. When we find a weakness in our spouse, we must accept that person as he or she is, because only on the basis of that acceptance can we draw out the partner's higher potential. If the desire to change the partner is rooted in love, we will then say only as much as can be truly helpful. We must never assume the role of guru in reforming our spouse's character or in instructing him or her in the art of living, because that places an intolerable strain on marriage."

If, for example, one's spouse doesn't meditate regularly and one would like to change that behavior, how can that best be communicated without evoking resistance?

Kriyananda: "It's always wise to carefully choose the moment when a truth can be communicated, and sometimes a lot of patience is required before the right moment comes. Then when you find a moment in which your spouse is receptive, seize it. Make sure that you aren't criticizing him or her and that your advice is humbly and tentatively offered, allowing your spouse the freedom to accept or reject your offering.

"For example, someone may visit your home who hasn't seen you in five years and comment, 'You look so peaceful and happy compared to five years ago.' You could explain that it's the result of regular meditation practice — and if your wife is present, she might ruminate over that. Later on she might approach you with the desire to meditate, and *that's* the moment, born of patience, in which change can occur."

How, then, is sexual expression to be viewed in a marriage in which the goal is self-realization?

Kriyananda: "All the scriptures say that the ideal is to sublimate the sexual energy into more creative and spiritual forms of expression.

"From an energy standpoint, all of life can be conceived of as energy expressing in varying degrees of refinement. As sexual energy is gradually transformed from passionate self-seeking into compassion and selfless service, the heart automatically unfolds and a higher, more spiritual love begins to manifest. In its highest degree of sublimation, redirected sexual energy can lift one's consciousness into the heights of superconsciousness, where one's individual soul merges in union with God, a state described in spiritual literature as the 'mystical marriage.' The bliss of sexual union on a physical level is infinitesimally small compared to the ecstasy of this higher union.

"Until our sexual nature is entirely brought under control and all our sexual energy is flowing upward toward God, it's best to follow the path of sexual moderation, which is the way of nature. Unfortunately, as we realize by looking around us, the way of society is to increase sexual desire and to follow the path of immoderation. The major cause of this imbalanced state is unnatural sexual excitation fueled by our toxic diets and by the constant sexual stimuli with which we're bombarded in our culture. In such an over-stimulated state, the sex center draws excessive energy to itself, demanding constant gratification.

"In the natural state, the sexual impulse demands less attention, and one doesn't make a big issue of it. One views it naturally — as an impulse rooted in nature but not to be indulged in excessively. Indeed, all sense pleasures are enhanced by moderation. This is as true of eating, partying, and good music as it is of sex. With excessive indulgence, what may have begun as enjoyment inevitably declines into the boredom of mere habit.''

If marriage partners agree, as an experiment in consciousness, to sublimate their sexual energies for the purpose of growth, wouldn't they be prone to feelings of guilt and failure if they couldn't live up to the spiritual ideal they set for themselves?

Kriyananda: "This is always possible, and that's why the saints throughout history have always acknowledged our right to be exactly where we are in our spiritual evolution. They always encourage us to grow in the recommended direction without doing injury to our nature. If a person is seeking complete and constant union with God, he must redirect all his energies Godward and follow Jesus' commandment to 'love the Lord thy God with all thy heart, and with all thy soul, and with all thy mind, and with all thy strength.' But until one has evolved to that state, progress must be made in moderate degrees.

"A worthy goal, then, is to experience sexual union with the attitude that the joy one feels comes from inside, as an internal communion of souls, rather than as an outward communion of bodies. Sex is spiritualized by learning to see God in the act and by concentrating more and more on His love flowing though you. There should be an inward consciousness of joy and communion with Him, a participation in God's infinite love, even while making love physically. With this awareness, little by little one will experience a level of sublimation developing naturally which would *never* come if one denied sexuality at the start for the purposes of enforced and unnatural growth."

Is there a technique you recommend to help couples channel sexual energy without setting up unnatural tensions in married life?

Kriyananda: "In general, the great spiritual teachers recommend selfless service as a way to purify the heart of selfish tendencies, and this 'technique' certainly applies in married life. By loving and serving another person — or God in the other person — totally and selflessly, we can transcend our narrow ego limitation, and that 'bridging' can lead into the universal experience of loving everybody. As married partners begin to channel their thought in the direction of serving each other and God, it soon becomes automatic for them not to seek pleasure merely for the purpose of self-gratification. They discover, instead, that the pleasure which comes from giving and serving far outweighs whatever they derive through self-seeking. For such a couple, sense moderation comes naturally, and opens the gates to higher consciousness.

"People who are excessively sexual are frequently nervous, irritable, and susceptible to ill health, depression, and lack of emotional control. They often suffer from diminished vitality and from premature aging. Those who live moderate, self-controlled, and balanced lives, on the other hand, have a luster in their eyes and a greater sense of joy and vitality in their movement. They radiate a health and well-being which come from redirecting and conserving sexual energy.

"If one has never discovered the health, well-being, and vigor that sexual moderation and control can bring, he can discover it for himself in the laboratory of his own life. The first toddling step in this endeavor is to redirect one's thinking, so that instead of *getting* for himself, he thinks constantly and habitually of *giving* to others."

Wouldn't this same attitude of selfless service apply to spiritual parenting as well?

Kriyananda: "Definitely. Children, perhaps even more than one's spouse, are incentives for one to relate in a giving way, forcing one to eschew the thought which is so instinctive to the immature ego: 'What's in it for me?' Because the child is so totally dependent, his parents must learn to give — and give and give! They must also learn to sublimate their own personal reaction to things, which in itself is a form of service. Parents can't afford to think, 'I don't like the fact that he's still wetting the bed.' They must redirect the focus of their thought and take the more selfless attitude, 'How can I help him overcome this problem?'

"The parent who allows personal irritation to cloud his treatment of his children fails both them and himself: them, because he will not treat them according to *their* needs; and himself, because he fails to see that his encounters with them are as much his opportunity as they are the children's. The parent who chooses to use parenting as a tool for spiritual growth — both his children's and his own — thinks not in terms of personal desire but of his children's needs. In this way, he learns to transcend his own petty ego concerns.

"Perhaps the great lesson that parents need to learn is to overcome the strong hypnosis which nature places upon parental consciousness, namely the thought, 'This is *my* child, an extension of myself.' If parents can get their egos out of the way and realize that their children have been given to them by God and that their divine task as parents is to serve the children in God's name, family life can be spiritualized into a form of *sadhana*, or spiritual discipline. Admittedly, it's hard to eliminate the thought, reinforced by nature, that 'This is *my* child,' but our task in spiritual life is to set aside all that which inclines us toward the delusion of ego, and to concentrate on those more expansive attitudes which conduce toward liberation in the Infinite. Child-raising, then, which for so many only reinforces their limited self-definition, can be used as a means of exploring our potential for self-transcendence."

So, in marriage and family life, we must first concentrate our focus, which then becomes a way for us to expand that focus into areas of universal concern.

Kriyananda: "Yes. It's good to concentrate our energies by being loyal to one person, one small group, one religion, one spiritual practice. Through that kind of concentration of life energy, we can reach a level of Divine attunement in which we see the same God in everyone and are able to love all

equally. If, in our effort to practice universal
love, we also concentrate on truly loving and
serving our spouse, we will eventually reach
that level of refined, impersonal love which is
divine Love."

Holy Vows at Marriage

I am thine, thou art mine, so that we may merge into God.

Body, mind, and soul we cast into the flame of love, to be purified into cosmic love for all mankind.

We will cooperate with each other so that we may harmonize with the laws of truth.

We will love each other so that we may know God's love.

We will merge our desires for the highest common good.

We will love each other unconditionally.

Through our love, we will forgive each other always.

We will love each other in order to be loyal to divine love.

May our half-souls join into the One Spirit of God.

We aspire to bring souls on earth to worship God as new-born souls.

May our children serve as spiritual ushers to bring other souls back from delusion's home into the eternal freedom in God.

May we love each other unselfishly, ever-increasingly, until our love becomes the love of God.

We are united by Spirit first, and by the bonds of our inner liking, mutual intellectual affinity, and physical attraction secondarily.

We will never cease to be friends, even if our bodies are parted by death or other separation.

We are united to fulfill the law of creation and, through our perfect love, to find the perfect love of God.

—PARAMHANSA YOGANANDA
Whispers from Eternity,
1949 *Edition*

About the Author

J. Donald Walters (who later received the monastic name Swami Kriyananda) was born in 1926 in Rumania, to American parents. He was educated in Rumania, Switzerland, England and the United States, viewing Western civilization from both sides of the ocean.

At an early age he decided to become an author and playwright, but later abandoned the ambition, not because he lacked ability, but because he felt unable to say anything truly *meaningful.*

In *The Path: Autobiography of a Western Yogi,* Swami Kriyananda describes his intense and moving search for meaning. This search culminated in 1948 when he met and became a direct disciple of Paramhansa Yogananda, the famous master of Yoga. For fourteen years he served his master's organization, Self-Realization Fellowship, as director of SRF centers around the world, principal teacher and lecturer, member of the Board of Directors, and first vice-president.

Having been instructed by Yogananda to serve others specifically through writing and teaching, Swami Kriyananda returned to his literary endeavors. Since 1962 he has written many books, short stories, plays and poems. Each of these approaches the question of life's deeper meaning from a different perspective: philosophy (*Crises in Modern Thought*); sociology (*Cooperative Communities*); economics (*The Road Ahead*); psychology and astrology (*Your Sun Sign as a Spiritual Guide*); art (*Meaning in the Arts*); drama and humor ("The Jewel in the Lotus"); and the classic science of yoga (*THE PATH*; *Yoga Postures for Self Awareness*; and *14 Steps to Perfect Joy*).

In addition to his writing, Swami Kriyananda is also well known for the power and quality of his voice, both as a speaker and a singer. A prolific composer, he has written original spiritual music for voice, piano and chorus. One of his current directions is "spiritualizing the arts."

In 1968 Swami Kriyananda founded Ananda Cooperative Village, one of the first and most successful new spiritual communities in the world. At present Swami lives at Ananda where he continues his work of writing and teaching. He also spends increasingly more time lecturing throughout North America and abroad.

HOW-TO-LIVE BOOKS

from Ananda Publications*

THE PATH: Autobiography of a Western Yogi.
Swami Kriyananda. 1977; 640 pp., photos.
ISBN: 0-916124-12-6, paper $4.95
ISBN: 0-916124-11-8, cloth $15.00

Internationally known as an author, lecturer, composer, and founder of Ananda Cooperative Village, Kriyananda tells the story of his life and the path that led him from his childhood in Europe and America to the feet of the great Indian Yoga master, Paramhansa Yogananda.

THE PATH gives a balanced overview of the spiritual life, for both the intellectually curious and the dedicated seeker.

THE SHORTENED PATH
Condensed by the author. 1981; 230 pp., photos.
ISBN: 0-916124-19-3, paper $6.95

---

*Available at book stores or order directly from Ananda Publications.

COOPERATIVE COMMUNITIES: How to Start Them and Why
Swami Kriyananda. 120 pp., photos.
ISBN: 0-916124-01-0, paper $4.95

The blueprint for a new lifestyle built on self-sufficiency, dignity, and simplicity. Text includes a history of communities, their social relevance in modern civilization, and guidelines for establishing a community enterprise. Also includes the story of Ananda Cooperative Village, one of the most successful intentional communities in the world.

Sharing Nature With Children
Joseph Bharat Cornell. 143 pp., illus.
ISBN: 0-916124-14-2, paper $4.95

A nature guide for teachers, parents, and counselors, recommended and used by Boy Scouts of America, National Audubon Society, National Science Teachers' Association, Girl Scouts of America.

Presents 42 games and activities designed to lead children into actual experiences with nature. Based on the principles that nature education should be simple, should involve direct experiences, and should teach values as well as facts.

How to Use Money For Your Own Highest Good
S. Kriyananda. ISBN: 0-916124-22-3, paper $2.95

Here are the keys to a perfectly balanced attitude toward money. You'll learn how to develop prosperity consciousness, how to maintain prosperity through money in the right way, how to gain and spend money rightly in order to grow spiritually.

Yoga Postures for Self Awareness
Swami Kriyananda. 102 pp., many photos.
ISBN: 0-916124-00-2, paper $4.95

A yoga primer that adds a whole new dimension to yoga practice. Its unique "awareness" approach teaches how to use body, mind, emotions, and spiritual nature for a more enjoyable life. Full-page photographs and clear instructions make this book perfect for beginners as well as yoga teachers.

The Art of Creative Leadership
S. Kriyananda. 16 pp.
ISBN: 0-916124-20-7, paper $2.00

A booklet of helpful rules based on the premise, "People are more important than things." Shows how you, as parent, teacher, friend, manager, can inspire others, bringing out their highest potential.

Your Sun Sign as a Spiritual Guide
Swami Kriyananda. 129 pp.
ISBN: 0-916124-02-9, paper $4.95

The use of astrology as originally intended—as a science for self-discovery. Analysis of each sign is presented in terms of developing one's highest potential. Opens up the spiritual dimension of astrological counselling.

Crises in Modern Thought
Swami Kriyananda. 248 pp.
ISBN: 0-916124-03-7, paper $4.95

A major contribution to the field of Western philosophy, *Crises in Modern Thought* confronts the modern challenge of meaninglessness with several daring challenges of its own. Without bias, Kriyananda examines nihilism, the relativity of values, the dethroning of Reason, the accidental nature of evolution, and the question of progress in evolution.

A Visit to Saints of India
Swami Kriyananda. 100 pp.
ISBN: 0-916124-06-1, paper $3.95

A pilgrimage through spiritual India with an experienced and insightful guide. Includes portraits of Sai Baba, Anandamayee Ma, Muktananda and others.

Stories of Mukunda
Swami Kriyananda. 110 pp., illus.
ISBN: 0-916124-09-6, paper $4.95

Inspiring stories from the boyhood of Paramhansa Yogananda, yoga master and author of the classic *Autobiography of a Yogi*. Suitable for children and adults.

The Divine Romance
Swami Kriyananda.
An original sonata in three movements for piano.
Sheet music. 11 pp., $2.50

Melodic beauty and a mood of spiritual inspiration combine to make *The Divine Romance* a unique and moving musical experience. Both amateur and professional pianists will find this outstanding piano composition a joy to play.

FOURTEEN STEPS TO PERFECT JOY: A Home-Study Correspondence Course in Yoga

This is what you receive:
I. **The Fourteen Steps Practice Manual**
II. **Cassette tape for each lesson**
III. **Personal guidance** through correspondence with a trained yoga teacher
IV. **Study Aids:** Swami Kriyananda's book, **Yoga Postures for Self Awareness,** with three additional tapes on yoga postures and meditation.

Please send for the free 26-page brochure.

HOW-TO-LIVE TAPES
from Ananda Recordings*

Making Your Marriage Work & Effective Child-Raising
two tapes, ST-5, $12.95

Here's the original tape from which this book was taken. Listening to the spoken words will help make a deeper impression on your memory. You can review the material as you drive to work or do other activities which don't demand full concentration.

Women's Role in Society Today
one tape, 45 minutes, SS-32, $7.95

Side One: Each person has both masculine and feminine qualities, and the goal is to balance the strengths of each. Kriyananda describes the importance of the female principle—intuition, compassion, and love—in a society which has gone too far in the direction of reason and intellectuality. *Side Two:* The importance of seeing God, not oneself, as the Doer.

How to Control Your Emotions
one tape, 85 minutes, SC-6, $8.95

This talk will help you understand how you can be more even-minded and happy; how you can overcome the pain that negative emotions cause. The tape ends with a lively question-and-answer session.

Send for the complete Ananda Recordings Catalog:
Ananda Recordings
Department MF
14618 Tyler Foote Road
Nevada City, CA 95959

916/292/3111

---

*Please include tape codes when placing your order.

NOTES